REVIVE & BUILD
LIKE EZRA

PRAY & BUILD
LIKE NEHEMIAH

WORKBOOK

A BIBLE STUDY WITH GROWTH ASSIGNMENTS
BY SHIRLEY A. FRANKLIN

Revive & Build Like Ezra, Pray & Build Like Nehemiah

Copyright 2023 by Shirley A. Franklin

All rights reserved. This book is protected by the copyright laws of the United States. No part of this book may be copied or reprinted for commercial gain or profit. The use of short quotes for personal or group study is permitted and encouraged.

Disclaimer: The publisher and author are providing this book and its contents on an "as is" basis and make no representations or warranties of any kind with respect to its book or contents. The content of this book is for informational purposes only. The publisher and author make no guarantees concerning the level of success you may experience by following the advice and strategies contained in this book, and you accept the risk that results will differ for each individual.

Writezous Publishing
301 S. Heatherwilde Blvd, #51
Pflugerville, Tx 78660-9998

ISBN: 978-0-9778520-6-2

Unless otherwise indicated, all Scripture references are taken from THE MESSAGE. Copyright 1993, 1994, 1995, 1996, 2000, 2001, 2002. Used by permission of NavPress Publishing Group.

Scripture quotations marked (NIV) are taken from the Holy Bible, New International Version®, NIV®. Copyright © 1973, 1978, 1984, 2011 by Biblica, Inc.™ Used by permission of Zondervan. All rights reserved worldwide. www.zondervan.com. The "NIV" and "New International Version" are trademarks registered in the United States Patent and Trademark Office by Biblica, Inc.™

Scripture quotations marked (NLT) are taken from the Holy Bible, New Living Translation, copyright ©1996, 2004, 2015 by Tyndale House Foundation. Used by permission of Tyndale House Publishers, Carol Stream, Illinois 60188. All rights reserved.

Scripture quotations marked (CEV) are from the Contemporary English Version Copyright © 1991, 1992, 1995 by American Bible Society. Used by Permission.

Scripture quotations marked (KJV) are from The Authorized (King James) Version. Rights in the Authorized Version in the United Kingdom are vested in the Crown. Reproduced by permission of the Crown's patentee, Cambridge University Press.

Scripture quotations marked (AMP) are taken from the Amplified® Bible, Copyright © 2015 by The Lockman Foundation. Used by permission. www.lockman.org"

Scripture quotations marked (ESV) are from The ESV® Bible (The Holy Bible, English Standard Version®), copyright © 2001 by Crossway, a publishing ministry of Good News Publishers. Used by permission. All rights reserved.

Cover and Book Design by Ashley E. Dowell

Table of Contents

1. Destiny Helpers — 7

2. Prayer, Strategy — 29

3. Distractions — 47

4. Reminding God — 59

5. Purifying Your Works — 71

6. Do It Afraid — 85

7. Revival/Revelations — 107

8. History — 117

9. Diligence/Due Diligence — 133

10. My Worship is the Real Deal — 151

Dedicated to my parents:
Doris Bell and Booker T. Franklin

For whatever was written in earlier times was written for our instruction, so that through endurance and the encouragement of the Scriptures we might have hope and overflow with confidence in His promises.

Romans 15:4 (AMP)

Chapter 1

Destiny Helpers

As we enter into this first chapter, I desire to address God-appointed destiny helpers. Destiny helpers could be defined as people who have the skill, abilities, connections, resources, materials, or something else that you need in order to fulfill an assignment, complete a project, reach a goal or properly answer a calling. It may be the case with you that, in spite of all of your skills, all of your blessings and all you possess, you are lacking in one or more areas or need divine support for what you're doing.

When you meditate on the fact that prayer and guidance are

needed for the proper determination and use of destiny helpers, there's no better example for us than Ezra; who supported the work of Nehemiah. Ezra was a key player in helping to get the Israelites back into a devoted relationship with God. His part of the project was to re-establish worship in Jerusalem after the Israelites came from exile in Babylon and rebuilding the Temple of God. The act of worshipping and the place for worshipping were his key parts.

Nehemiah was the one who instituted the rebuilding project, as pertains to the walls and the gates in Jerusalem. Both of these men played an integral role in doing what was necessary after the Israelites were released from captivity. But without Ezra, Nehemiah's work would not have been as complete or as anointed, nor would it have been finished in record time as was the case.

Since they faced perpetual challenges and threats – prayer and corporate worship were key factors. Give that some thought. Reflect upon the fact that there are things that you need to re-establish in your life. What is that/those thing(s)? What is missing when it seems that you have everything that you need? You might reach a point where you realize and identify something like the forthcoming examples are missing.

Like Nehemiah and Ezra, once you identify what you need that is outside of your wheelhouse or ability, that's when you need a destiny helper - a person like Ezra is ideal because this scholar and priest knew the word of God. He was well-versed in the scriptures and familiar with the protocols for worship. In addition, chapter 7 of the book of Ezra details the favor he'd received to get the king's support. This included issuing binding decrees, giving authorization, issuing orders for provisions and communicating with advisors and officials to back him up. He sent word ahead of Ezra. Furthermore, Ezra was the person God dispatched at the right time to prepare the Israelites to join the work of Nehemiah.

As Ezra was laden with all this and with a heart to see Jerusalem restored, it provided confirmation that he was a hand-picked destiny helper for Nehemiah. They were on one accord - another confirmation. This is critical for any undertaking, especially those of mass scale. They agreed that Jerusalem needed to be restored to its former glory. The power of agreement and being in one accord is found in Matthew 18:20, and the outcome is found in John 17:11b-19, where it reads that God commands a blessing for unity. Even during the building of the Tower of Babel, the Lord said that with unity nothing was impossible for man (Genesis 11:6).

Your destiny helpers will have the right credentials and authority to assist you just like Ezra did for Nehemiah. Your destiny helpers will be of one mind (in unity) and in agreement with you.

Ezra read the scriptures every day before the people that were involved in the rebuilding project. They had a solemn assembly. This occurred before they started rebuilding each day. It's like you see in a relay race. In this instance, Ezra held the baton and ran the first leg, and then symbolically passed the baton to Nehemiah.

Your destiny helper(s) should be a person/people of prayer. In the book of Ezra, it mentions in chapter 1 that a proclamation was issued by King Cyrus. It specified that Ezra would help build a Temple for the Lord, a temple of worship in Jerusalem. The king gave his full and rich blessings to Ezra for this project.

In Hebrew 6:12, the writer tells the early Christians, "Be like (follow after) those who stay the course with committed faith and then get everything promised to them."

Once again the Israelites were coming out of captivity and out of exile so, to re-establish worship and make that a priority as well as to build a temple of worship was important as anything else that was taking place. King Cyrus also turned over all the vessels and utensils from the Temple of God which had been taken while God's people were in captivity.

Chapter 3 narrates the beginning of the temple rebuilding project, and then in chapter 4 we see that they had to stop. Rebuilding resumed in chapter 5. Ezra is by no means the only one who had the authority to do something and then was forced to stop before continuing. See if this applies to you - have you backslidden or have you stopped attending church, or if you go less often or have a lower level of involvement when you go or used to participate in the street ministry devoted to winning souls but no longer do that. Any of these could still count as backsliding. Think about whether there's something like this that you have stopped. Both service and worship are important. Do you do those with the same measure as before? It's important that worship takes place in a certain way. The Lord says, in spirit and in truth. Is that how you worship the Holy and Altogether Righteous God? That is how He wants us worshipping him, his requirement or standard.

If you are needing an Ezra in your life, think about that person that is consistent about their worship, has a dynamic prayer life and lives in a consistently Christian way that you aspire to likewise live. Think about that person that is loving, living Godly and is willing to possibly be an accountability partner for you and also would be a potential destiny helper. You need to see certain qualities in that person and receive confirmation after seeking God about it.

Give some deep thought to what kind of qualities you would want in a mentor type of destiny helper. Let Ezra be your guide. A person who you're giving some of your power over to, and that you're humble enough to allow to remind you of commitments you make or conditions for their help. Will they be able to commit to holding you accountable for being faithful in that area that slipped - the area of accountability?

Here's a positive point. Accountability partners that really love you and want to see you win will show their love by helping you be your best self, to be more Christ-like. They can help you grow by leaps and bounds and achieve your goals, faster. The right one can spur you to greater success and to re-establishing your footing in an area where you have slipped. When you are trying to restore something lost or discontinued for whatever reason, a destiny helper can aid you in this.

For instance, you could even be a person who had a job that required you to work on Sundays, and that's why you have not been to church for a while. Take an honest look at the things in your life. If attending church is not the problem, ask yourself whether you might indeed go to church, but you're not fully engaged when you're there. Do you go to church just out of habit or do you go to church number one, to serve and number two to be fed, number three to be inspired number four to worship in an assembly with other Christians?

Continuing, there is number 5, to have your iron sharpened through exposure and right dividing of the Word. Number six for fellowship with other believers.

When you go to church, those should be some of the things that you're looking for. Is there any area that I mentioned that you are not as diligent about when you go to church? I suggest that you be intentional the next time that you get ready for church. One good idea to help with this is to play worship songs while you're getting ready after you've awakened. Next, be already prayed up, be already in a good, positive spirit. Spend time with the Lord before you interact with even the people in the same room with you or in your household.

Next, as you are heading for church, keep your spirit calm and in a right alignment with God. Another idea is to play worship music and/or spend more time meditating on God's word as you're on your way to church. This is important - no matter what may happen; including bad traffic, the wrong kinds of interactions with other drivers, a frowning face, or a person who is in another car playing loud, worldly music with the windows down while you're trying to keep your spirit right, someone in the car with you cutting up - let none of those things move you.

Of course, once you get into the house of the Lord, do as David did. He said, "I will enter his gates with thanksgiving and into his courts with praise." (Ps. 100:4) Do you do that?

I penned this particular chapter with the aim of helping you to commit to allowing destiny helpers, accountability partners who should have mastered the area(s) where you still struggle. This includes returning to true worship. I feel compelled to really provoke you toward the cause of being faithful in attending a good Bible-believing Jesus exalting church. Doing it consistently with the right spirit while having an accountability partner who has achieved these milestones to help you in that regard is important. If your prayer life or your study of the word is not as good as you would like to be, accountability partners could be one of the following:

1. A bible study leader

2. A minister that is not really

active in the pulpit but is in training to become a seminarian or going to some type of Bible college or through a Christian leadership program.

Such a person could be found in joining something like a Bible Study Fellowship (BSF), where you get together with other women or men and study certain sections of the Bible.

Outside of having helpers, mentors and accountability partners, you can investigate doing some of the following things on your own:

• Getting a Bible that has a Concordance can be a great source of reference to help you. These study bibles are available in different translations. You can grow spiritually if you have the right kind of Bible and Bible Study resources.

Take a look at whether you have the right Bible for deeper Bible Study. Deeper exploration in studying the Bible will help you to grow.

• Consider purchasing or referencing (online or otherwise) The Amplified version of the Bible. That particular Bible has expanded elements for the scriptures. One example of what I mean is in I Peter 5:7, where it says, "Cast your care upon him for he cares for you," in another version. That's really wonderful, reasonably clear and it's very reassuring, but in the Amplified Bible it says, "Cast the whole of your cares, [all of your anxieties, all of your worries, and all your concerns once and for all] on Him, for He cares about you [with deepest affection, and watches over you very carefully"]. (AMP)

With that amplification or expansion on some of the ways that clarify what that scripture means, you can gain a better, deeper understanding of the scriptures.

Designate a private place (ideally on a wall or in a closet, in whole or in part) where you can write down key scriptures and write down prayers and return to them through journaling. When you put a petition before God, write down the date you made that petition and then go back later and write down when the prayer was answered.

Your homework before you go on to the next chapter is as follows:

Brainstorm to write a list of possible people who God may assign to you in terms of a destiny helper or helpers for you. Notice how Ezra and Nehemiah were aligned – and seek such alignment between you and the person. Bible study teachers may be able to point out a potential helper candidate for you. They remain a candidate only until you pray, and then ask them for the assistance you need. While they are still a candidate, write their names down, and observe them to see if they pass the litmus tests in the areas that I mentioned. See Hebrews 6:12 which I highlighted earlier. Such people will hold your feet to the fire, sharpen you and help you get where you're supposed to be in your walk with God. Prayerfully seek the right person and approach them to request their help, after you've completed the other steps. I believe God will show you who to approach to help you arrive at your goal, your destiny, your destination.

After that look at making an upgrade of some resources to enhance your Bible study time and your worship time. Then ponder how you prepare yourself before going to church. Next, ponder exactly how you prepare yourself for prayer and bible study. Lastly, say a prayer to ask God to help you to improve your heart posture - to purify your heart.

In all honesty, Nehemiah could as easily be seen as Ezra's destiny helper. Their roles were complementary and symbiotic. More importantly, remember that Jesus is the best role model anyone can have.

Homework
Growth Assignment

Date_____

For whatever was written in earlier times was written for our instruction, so that through endurance and the encouragement of the Scriptures we might have hope and overflow with confidence in His promises.

Romans 15:4 (AMP)

Chapter 2

Prayer, Strategy

We looked briefly at Ezra in the first chapter. You can think of him as a revivalist who was both a prophet and a priest. The book of Nehemiah comes right after the Book of Ezra and just before the Book of Esther. This placement should make it easy for you to use this book and toggle back and forth between the two books, Ezra and Nehemiah, to look at most scripture references and complete the homework in each chapter.

Chapter 1, starting with verse 1 of Nehemiah, tells details of how Nehemiah found out from someone he knew who had just arrived from Judea with some fellow Jews that the exile survivors who were left there in the province were in bad shape – in a state of disgrace. According to the report, conditions were appalling, the walls of Jerusalem were still rubble, and the city gates were still in cinders. It recounts Nehemiah's words in verse 4 - "When I heard this, I sat down and wept, I mourned for days, fasting and praying before the God of heaven. I said 'God of Heaven, the Great and Awesome God, loyal to his covenant and faithful to those who love him and obey his commands, look at me, listen to me, pay attention to this prayer of your servant that I'm praying day and night in intercession for your servants, the people of Israel, confessing the sins of the people of Israel, and I'm including myself, I and my ancestors among those who have sinned against you.'"

He continues praying in verse 7, "We've treated you like dirt. We haven't done what you told us, haven't followed your commands, and haven't respected the decisions you gave to Moses, your servant." This former cupbearer goes on and he even reminds himself in this prayer as he continues speaking to God Almighty, "We know we are the ones that are in the wrong. We are the ones that have acted up." Skipping down to verses 10-11 he says: "Well, there they are, your servants, your people whom you so powerfully and impressively redeemed, O Master, listen to me, listen to your servants, prayer and yes, to all your servants who did right in honoring you and make me successful today, so that get what I want from the king." He identifies his role with the words: "I was the king's cup-bearer."

God answered that prayer and the king gave him a passport, (so to speak), a letter, supplies, and other provisions. In chapter 2 verses 8-9, it says, "The generous hand of my God was with me in this and the king gave to me what I asked. When I met the governors across the river, meaning the Euphrates, I showed them the king's letters. The king even sent along a Calvary escort."

Just like Ezra, Nehemiah got what he needed from the king. Proverbs 21:1 tells us, "The King's heart is in the hands of the Lord, and he turns it however he might." Some versions say that God turns it like one would turn the waters of a river. On USGS.gov it indicates that rivers are formed by water moving from a higher height to a lower height because of the gravitational pull until the river flow joins with the ocean, gets diverted, is lapped up by thirsty creatures, seeps into the ground, or evaporates. That's a lot of movement.

God's hands can do similarly with the king's heart, moving it as he desires for a multitude of reasons or purposes. Just like he hardened Pharaoh's heart when Moses went before him, he can be credited with softening King Cyrus' and King Artaxerxes' hearts so that Jerusalem could be returned to its former glory.

Nehemiah went to rebuild after he got what he needed, sort of like an approved leave of absence from his job. It says in chapters 2 and 4 that there was a man named Sanballat who got very angry that someone was coming to look after the benefit of the people of Israel - God's chosen.

When Nehemiah arrived back home, it was not without some friction, because there were other men that also did not want this rebuilding to take place. In spite of the fact that Nehemiah kept silent about his mission, somehow they heard about it, and so they tried to oppose him and his team.

The Troublesome Trio - Sanballat, Tobias, and Geshem did all kinds of things to try and distract them, try to stop them, attempt to intimidate them, arrange to threaten them, convince them to come down and hide or come down to meet with them. However, what we see in the book of Nehemiah is that they did not stop building. Their mission of rebuilding the walls and the gate continued without wavering. They also prayed, with both Ezra and Nehemiah playing a key role in this. In Chapter 2 verse 20 are Nehemiah's words. "I shot back, 'The God of Heaven will make sure we succeed. We're his servants and we're going to work, rebuilding. You can stick to your own business. You get no say in this. Jerusalem's none of your business.'"

That's what he said in response to these troublesome Ammonite government officials. Just as Nehemiah said, they were not stakeholders in the rebuilding project.

The key points that I want you to look at it from here are:

1. That you can continue to make prayer in the midst of trouble.

2. You can also complete assignments strategically and with fidelity the way Nehemiah did.

Key Verses:

Nehemiah 4:9, "We countered with prayer to our God and set a round-the-clock guard against them."

Ezra 7:10, "Ezra had committed himself to studying the Revelation of God, to living it, and to teaching Israel to live its truths and ways."

Pearls of Wisdom:

Look how Nehemiah continued to make prayer his priority when all of these rumblings; complaints; threats; intimidations and distractions were swirling all around him. An example of that is also found in Chapter 2 and elsewhere. He even prayed a short prayer in chapter

6:9b, "Give me strength."

Time and time again, Nehemiah met the challenges with prayer. It says in Chapter 4, verses 4-5 that Nehemiah prayed, "Oh, listen to us, dear God. We're so despised: Boomerang their ridicule on their head; have their enemies cart them off as war trophies to a land of no return; don't forgive their iniquity, don't wipe away their sin – they've insulted the builders."

He reported, "We kept at it, repairing and rebuilding the wall. The whole wall was soon joined together and halfway to its intended height, because the people had a heart for the work." Another way of saying that people had a heart for the work is that the people were diligent. If you were to look up the definition of diligent you would find words that indicate being steadfast and unmovable and devoted to doing quality work - not being idle.

Today, we sometimes hear the word slackers to describe people who are not diligent in their work. I wonder how many slackers are slackers because they lack the strategy and steps for doing the work assigned to them. I wonder if they are slackers because they don't have a vision or haven't caught the vision.

Since we explore diligence in greater detail in another chapter, I want you to think about what I call, "The Glorious In-between" found in the work of Nehemiah.

The last thing I want to talk about in this chapter is strategy. From the book of Nehemiah we can see that with prayer, Nehemiah was able to receive ideas and specific strategies to help with the rebuilding project. He executed those strategies with excellence.

A strategy can be defined as a method or a system for doing something or accomplishing something. In the 4th chapter of Nehemiah in verses 13 and 14 after they had experienced some report that their dedicated enemies were saying certain things and even gathering around them; some trying to surround them to attack, Nehemiah reported, "So I stationed armed guards at the most vulnerable pace places of the wall. And assigned people by families with their swords, lances, and bows. After looking over things I stood up and spoke to the nobles, officials, and everyone. 'Don't be afraid of them. Put your mind on the master Great and awesome, and then fight for your brothers, your sons, your daughters or wives, and your homes.'" (paraphrased from Nehemiah 4:13-14). He spurred them on by pointing out their personal familial attachment and the expected end of their efforts.

As you read on, you will find those next verses detail how common laborers held a tool in one hand and a spear in the other. Then each of the builders had a sword strapped to their side as they worked. And then Nehemiah himself kept the trumpeter at his side to sound the alert if necessary. These groups used one hand to build and had one hand prepared to fight.

Time and time again, we see specific strategies that he used for rebuilding. He was like the superintendent or foreman that we see in building projects today. You can read many verses that describe what each person or group did in the rebuilding of the gates and other parts. What Nehemiah did was basically assigned people designated territories in the rebuilding project. He even had a specific formation for them to use (Neh. 3).

Additionally, he stationed armed guards, as we see in chapter 4, because the troublesome trio was still at it, and several other enemies of God's people were super determined to keep them from getting things back to normal. He even made sure that no one was covering the same area, by giving specific boundaries, sections, and locations for each person's work (Neh. 4:13, 16-22). You can think of this as efficient leadership.

I've worked jobs where one person

in leadership did not meet or communicate efficiently with another leader, and they each either told me two different strategies to implement to address an issue, or they had me in two separate mandatory meetings to tell me the same exact thing. That was neither efficient nor effective. My point is that strategy and steps to implement it can help be efficient, avoid wasting time, and be efficiently victorious like Nehemiah. Nehemiah 6:15 indicates that they finished in record time - 52 days.

Your homework before going to the next chapter is to determine for which area(s) you want to ask God to give you a strategy and steps. Write them down on your Growth Assignment page. Once you have that, seek God in prayer. Ask him to help you find out a strategy and steps that you can use for victory in a particular area. This could be on your job, in your business, in your home in your relationships, in your business, or in raising your children.

Write down the date you asked. When you receive what you asked for, write down the date that it manifests and how it manifests. I believe God is faithful and will give you the strategy and steps for winning. After that, your work is to use the strategy and steps that God gives you. Do it with fidelity and give all praises unto God when you see the outcome (signs following) of obeying His customized directions.

Homework
Growth Assignment

Date_____

For whatever was written in earlier times was written for our instruction, so that through endurance and the encouragement of the Scriptures we might have hope and overflow with confidence in His promises.

Romans 15:4 (AMP)

Chapter 3

Distractions

In this chapter, I want to address distractions. Someone once said, "If Satan can't steal your joy he will definitely try to distract you," and "If Satan can't have your heart, he will certainly try to distract you." Someone else said, "If the enemy can't destroy you, he will try to distract you." Additionally, one uncredited quote says, "Don't let the noise of the world distract you from God." Mark Zuckerberg, the creator of Facebook, probably knows a lot about managing distractions. He is credited with saying, "I'm here to build something for the long term. Anything else is a distraction."

Winston Churchill said, "You will never reach your destination if you stop and throw stones at every dog that bites." Another person said, "When the enemy sends distractions, they don't look like distractions until he's been successful at distracting you." In Philippians 13:13-14 the apostle Paul wrote, "Keep your eyes on Jesus, who both began and will finish this race we're in. Study how he did it, because he never lost sight of where he was headed, that exhilarating finish line with God. He could put up with anything along the way, cross, shame, whatever, and now he's there, in the place of Honor right alongside God Almighty. And when you find yourself flagging in your face, go over that story again, item by item, that long litany of hostility, he pulled through. That will shoot adrenaline into your soul."

There are many scriptures that instruct us to keep or turn our attention/eyes on Jesus. When you hear it in songs like, "Turn Your Eyes On Jesus" by Helen Howarth Lemmel, it is basically reminding you not to be distracted. Don't be distracted during prayer. Don't be distracted when you're reading the Bible. Don't be distracted at church. Don't be distracted when God is speaking to your heart about some matter. Don't be distracted when you're meditating on God's word. The enemy does operate through distractions, and once again, they can be distractions that don't seem to be distractions.

I really want to encourage you to take an honest look at these things in your life: Where are you being distracted?

Have you settled it in your heart that the enemy is going to try to use distractions?

My aim is for you to recognize that when we have that knowledge and we operate according to that knowledge we will do a whole lot better in managing those distractions over time, and eventually eliminating them. I feel compelled to really call forth all distractions that may exist in your life that could be easily besetting you.

Key Verse:

Nehemiah 6:3a – "I am engaged in a great work, so I can't come down." (NLT)

Pearls of Wisdom:

You can speak (out loud) to your distractions with words that cater to the situation and to the thing trying to distract you. Here is one example: "I need to stay in this Word so I can grow and know how to better handle situations. I can't check my social media posts now." You should practice this system to get yourself redirected to whatever you should be doing at the moment.

So, your homework before you go on to the next chapter is to first read and meditate on Nehemiah 6:3a. This is our key verse. You will then write on an index card in your workspace or War Room the words, "I'm doing a great work and I can't come down." (ESV) or another translation of the same verse.

As for me, I'm putting it on my voicemail. You can do it too!

Next, you will look up and write

down on the Homework Growth Assignment Page that follows - Proverbs 4:22-25. Also, write down 1 Peter 5:8. Please include the verse about Peter when he was walking on water as he headed to Jesus, as found in Matthew 12:28-30. You may recall that when he began to walk on the water he was doing fine until he became distracted by the winds and the waves.

I want you to meditate on those scriptures. And keep them before your eyes in some fashion. You can also copy them on index cards or sticky notes or somewhere where you can see them regularly and begin to identify things that operate as distractions in your own life. Begin to read them out loud on a daily basis.

Next, you will identify your distractions, and write them down. Your next step from there is long-term - you will work on not letting yourself be distracted again in the same way; as well as in the other ways that distractions come. You can say to yourself something similar to Nehemiah's, "I'm doing a great work and I can't come down." Reword it to suit the situation. Examples include, "I am studying to show myself approved, so I can't stop. Checking my emails can wait." (for Bible study), or "I am in the throne room/war room/behind the veil, in God's presence, and I can't waste this precious valuable time. I will eat a snack after I am finished," (when in prayer). See the pearl of wisdom earlier in this chapter to gain better insight into how this works and to view an additional example.

Lastly, find six quotes about distractions and write them down on your homework growth assignment page. Review them once per week.

This involves discipline and it's a bit demanding - but you can do it. The fruit of this change will be amazing to behold. I believe it will become part of your testimony.

Homework
Growth Assignment

Date_____

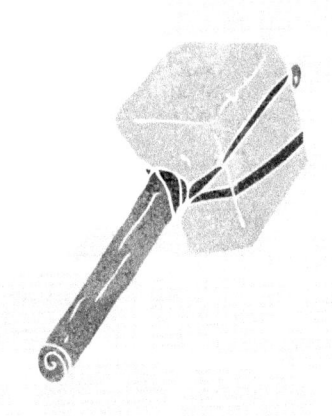

Chapter 4

Reminding God

In this chapter, I want to address reminding God of the works that you did for his name's sake - plus remembering the past. You might think, why would I want to remember the past? Let me share when this might be relevant using the books of Nehemiah and Ezra (our book pair) to share where there are times when these men thought it fitting to remember and even rehearse what they and their ancestors did that was wrong. I wrote earlier about how Ezra talked to the people forbidding intermarrying and being unequally yoked, but they did it anyway with leaders also participating. Ezra went to God and recounted their rebellious past and God's faithfulness in Ezra 9:6-15 after ripping his clothes, pulling his hair, and dropping to the ground. (Ezra 9:5).

Let's also take a look at the book of Nehemiah in the final chapter which is chapter 13 verses 15-16. This takes place after the walls and gates had been rebuilt and people were setting up their households. It was through those very gates that traders brought in sacks of grain and loaded their goods upon donkeys. They brought wine grapes, pigs, and all kinds of stuff to sell in Judah. They also brought in fish.

In verses 17-19, we find Nehemiah's reaction to their disobedience when he discovered that traders and dealers of goods brought these things into the gates of Judah to sell. Nehemiah says, "I confronted the leaders of Judah, "What's going on here? This evil. Profaning the Sabbath. Isn't this exactly what your ancestors did? And because of it, didn't God bring down on us and this city all this misery? And here you are adding to it, accumulating more wrath on Jerusalem by profaning the Sabbath." (Nehemiah 13:18).

As the day drew to a close in verse 19 Nehemiah goes on to say, "As the gates of Jerusalem were darkened by the shadows of the approaching Sabbath, I ordered the door shut and not to be open until the Sabbath was over, and placed some of my servants at the gate to make sure that nothing to be sold would get in on the Sabbath Day." (Nehemiah 13:19)

When I was growing up, there was a time when you could not purchase certain things on Sundays at the grocery store due to Blue Laws in Texas. They literally had certain sections of the store closed off with ropes and similar barricades. You could not purchase liquor, but there were other items that you could not buy on that day. I know that now you can buy anything - anywhere - anytime without any problem.

I executed this segment, this last chapter, with the aim of helping you to examine with fresh eyes how you are treating the Sabbath, first of all. I also want you to examine with laser-focus, on reminding God what you've done to the glory of his name as did Nehemiah on several occasions. Three instances of this show up in chapter 13.

Key Verses:

In Neh. 13:14, Nehemiah prayed a prayer of remembrance to God. "Remember me, Oh my God, for this. Don't ever forget the devoted work I have done for The Temple of God and its worship."

In Neh. 13:22, he entreated God by praying, "Remember me also for this, my God. Treat me with mercy, according to your great and steadfast love."

Lastly, in Neh. 13:31b, where he said, "Remember me, O my God, for good."

A positive point of focus is that he used the very personal words, "My God," in each of these prayers.

Pearls of Wisdom:

One of the hidden pearls that I

want to share is that God Almighty sees everything that you do. He has something called the Book of Life (Revelation 20:15) where He writes down everything the elect of God does. There is also The Book of Remembrance, referenced in Malachi 3:16-18.

Most likely, like Nehemiah, you would like God to remember you and your good works – the things you do in His name, for Him, to glorify Him. I am certain that you know that one day you will stand before him and he will say, (or at least you want him to say), "Good work! You did your job well. From now on be my partner," instead of, "Throw him into utter darkness." (Matthew 25:21, 26).

That's on a general basis. But on a specific basis take a moment to pinpoint something that you want

God to remember right now. Search your recent history and find something very positive and praiseworthy, something which is good and honorable. I can think of myself as an example if you will. I have worked in Special Education for the last few years after many years in Regular Education. If I were to say something to the Lord right now, I would say, "Lord Father, my God, Lord God in heaven, please remember the lavish love that I showed toward my students including how I bent over backward to build their confidence this year and help them to understand that they have just as much right as anyone else in their classes to understand the lesson content. Lord, my God, remember how I taught them how to raise their hands high and how to phrase specific questions, rather than saying,

"I'm confused", "I don't understand", or "You have made me feel confused." Remember how I taught them to say things like, "Can you repeat what you just said about inequalities, or can you show us another example of that, or can you give me a synonym of that word or explain it with different words? Lord, I want to remember that I taught them to self-advocate." Enough about me.

Your homework and the logic of the assignment, before you go to the next chapter, are as follows – I want to spur you to come up with some things that you want to remind God of that you did for his sake. Write a paragraph of prayer with your 3 things and begin each of the 3 things with the words like the one below or similar words,

"Lord, remember me for

_____", then you provide the rest of each sentence with your acts and works deemed worth reminding God about.

Homework
Growth Assignment

Date_____

For whatever was written in earlier times was written for our instruction, so that through endurance and the encouragement of the Scriptures we might have hope and overflow with confidence in His promises.

Romans 15:4 (AMP)

Chapter 5

Purifying Your Works

In this chapter, I want to emphasize the attention to detail and purifying that followed the completion of the rebuilding project in our book pair. In particular, I want to point out how Nehemiah was faithful in going to God and seeking his face consistently. During the building of the walls and gates of Jerusalem as mentioned in Chapter 13 verse 14, it's recorded that Nehemiah said in a prayer, "Remember me, oh my God, for this don't ever forget the devoted work I have done for the Temple of God and its worship." In the previous chapter verses 27-30 indicate that there was a dedication of the wall, gates, and the people. These verses recount how the priest ceremonially purified themselves. Then they did the same for the people, the gates, and the wall. This is about purifying their work and themselves.

As we are Christians of the New Covenant, we don't need human priests as described in these verses. I Peter 2:9 declares that we are a royal priesthood. I want you to take a look at where you can purify your work. Once you have completed a work for God how can you consecrate that, purify it, sanctify it, and make it clean or cleaner and more holy?

As an example - in some of my work as an author, when I'm writing a book some of my necessary purification includes editing and proofreading that book so I can publish it in a spirit of excellence.

I purify it by fixing the grammar, spelling, and syntax. I purify it by citing my references properly. I don't want the book launched with a lot of typographical errors, spelling errors, or improper grammar. Anything that could be distracting to the readers or that would diminish the quality of the book gets fixed during editing and proofreading. If I find that I am using certain words too much, I replace them with synonyms.

If you are involved or assigned some endeavor and you complete it, how can you purify that work even further? It may be the case that you had never thought about purifying your work. You're probably in good company.

Potentially you might be, as an example, a school janitor. It's important to work in any company with a brick-and-mortar location. Cleaning is noble work if it's done nobly. Perhaps after you sweep the floors you might have to scrub gum off the floor, and you might have to erase tennis shoe marks that may show up on the floor because student shoe bottoms that have black souls or even colored soles have scuffed the floor. On a rainy day, those shoes have mud, which gets tracked all over the building, as a janitor, you might have to also mop that floor. This is just one example of purifying the work of cleaning the floor in a way that makes it even better. It involves taking it a step or more further.

Enhancement is another way of thinking about purifying your work. Next, we'll use the example of a cook. When you put the food on the plate, and everything is cooked the way it should be with all the right seasonings and everything, purifying it might just mean that once it's on the plate you get a paper towel and wipe up the splatters all around the plate. In other words, you might purify it by making the presentation of the food look better. This could apply even if you will be the one eating from that plate.

There are many other examples other than the ones I provide. You should ask yourself how you could purify the work that you do.

Key Verse:

Nehemiah 12:30: "The priests and Levites held special ceremonies to make themselves holy, and then they did the same for the rest of the people and for the gates and walls of the city." (CEV)

Pearls of Wisdom:

A pearl of wisdom that I found in the Online Encyclopedia Britannia indicates that the Levites were musicians, gatekeepers, guardians, Temple officials, judges, and craftsmen who were service workers in public worship.

Here's one more hidden pearl of wisdom. God continually sanctifies us, consecrates us, and purifies us. He is a holy God and we are his people, and we should bear his likeness. A positive point here is that sanctification/purification is a process, and it doesn't happen overnight. So, you should not feel condemned if you are still in the early stages of understanding how sanctification and consecration, and purification apply to you in your life. Reading the Word is one way to become sanctified by the

Lord. Verses about purification appear in II Corinthians 7:1, Psalm 51:10, I John 1:9, and Titus 2:14.

Take an honest look at the things that happen in your home. Purification is something that can also be reflected in the appearance of our homes. What would enable your bookshelf books on your bookshelf to look better and more organized? I bring this up because I recently recognized that my bookshelf needs bookends to make it look tidier by holding the books upright.

What about the papers and the mail that you receive? Can you organize mail so your environment looks more presentable when it first comes into your home? Would a tiny shredder and tiny trash bin near the place where you store/sort mail prompt you to shred fliers and discard things you don't want to keep?

What might make the bathroom towels that are folded helter-skelter look more nice, fluffy, and appealing? What kind of basket or file organizers might make it easier for you to organize and establish a nice, neat orderly home environment?

I penned this chapter intending to help you to see the importance of purification of yourself and your work and to highlight how dedication for incremental results might help you increase your excellence at doing your work.

I want to provoke you toward continuous improvement in the things assigned to your hands. My prayer is that you don't fall into a state of laxity. I'm not saying that things should be done perfectly or look perfect. I'm saying, are you doing things with the spirit of excellence? Is there a high standard that you aim for in areas of your life?

Your homework before going to the next chapter is to list five ways or five places where you can purify your work. This may seem to be a simpler homework assignment compared to the others, but I want you to take it very seriously. If you have to meditate on those five areas needing a purifying touch, by all means, do so. Put certain ways/places that need your purifying touch on a calendar that you often look at so you have a greater chance of doing as you decide. Write it down, commit to it, and see what a difference it makes in your life.

Once you are finished, dedicate your work to the Lord. I want you to add this step because when you do your work in the spirit of excellence, you should be happy with your results and want to dedicate it to God.

Homework
Growth Assignment

Date_____

For whatever was written in earlier times was written for our instruction, so that through endurance and the encouragement of the Scriptures we might have hope and overflow with confidence in His promises.

Romans 15:4 (AMP)

Chapter 6

Do It Afraid

In this chapter, I want to dive into how to do your assigned work or necessary activity while afraid. In the book of Ezra, chapter 3, beginning with verse 3 it says even though they were afraid of what their non-Israeli neighbors might do, they went ahead anyway and set up the altar on its foundations and offered whole burnt offerings on it, morning and evening.

What we have here is some opposition to the God-ordained work, which included getting the Israelites back into devoted worship and rebuilding the Temple of God on Ezra's part. It occurred in a similar way that Nehemiah experienced opposition to the rebuilding of the walls and the gates of Jerusalem.

There are some indications that they might not be able to finish without a lot of opposition, a lot of naysayers, haters (of Jerusalem and the Israelites), and unfriendly neighbors after they returned from Babylonian captivity.

Ezra and those accompanying him were at the point where the foundation had not even been laid, and as you know, the foundation of any building is the part that is very close to the ground that builders build up from. If you can just imagine, the foundation is that very first level underneath the first level of a building that gives it the stability that has to be lain before the other building steps take place. The point here is that they were not even finished with the foundation, this early step, when they offered burnt offerings to the Lord and gave money to pay for specialist builders (Ez. 8:6-7). They were admittedly afraid of the neighbors. There were different reasons why they were afraid. Their enemies did not want worship taking place, did not want the ruins rebuilt, did not want people and families back together again, and did not want the Word of God to go forth.

Nonetheless, the Israelites continued celebrating and making offerings. They did it morning and evening, as the scripture I mentioned indicates. Once again, they did all that they did while afraid. They did it amid the different schemes being boldly carried out right under their noses.

Pearls of Wisdom:

One pearl of wisdom is that we should not wait until we're finished with something before we begin to celebrate and do the things that we know to do like worship, give of our time, talents, etc.

If you look further down in chapter 3, verse 7, it indicates that they donated money to hire the specialists that they needed. Then verse 6 says they began offering whole burnt offerings to God. We have two points or takeaways from this portion of the book of Ezra.

Rehearsing those points includes the following:

1. Sometimes you have to do the work assigned to you while afraid.

2. You can celebrate and get into

compliance with the principles that you know and have been taught. You don't have to wait until you're finished. You can go ahead and apply principles and celebrate even before you're finished.

This chapter focuses primarily on helping you to explore how fear limits and otherwise impacts our lives. Our lives need to be rich with worship and reading of the scriptures. We should be a people who serve and worship in a certain way, which is the way that is pleasing to God. He's made that known to us (from the deep wellspring of the heart, in sincerity and with gratitude – paraphrased from John 4:23-24).

What is it that you are afraid of, but nevertheless understand that it needs to be done? Think about it.

In trying to identify or pinpoint what are you fearful of, ask yourself, "What was the first thing that's top of mind for you?" Don't overthink it.

Pearls of Wisdom:

Here is one hidden pearl of wisdom straight from the Bible - II Timothy 1:7. "For God hath not given us the spirit of fear; but of power, and of love and of a sound mind." (KJV) Sometimes overcoming fear is a journey.

Now, I will give you an example from my personal life. I was involved in a very bad car accident where my vehicle, a 4-door sedan, went across three lanes of traffic after I got hit from behind by an extended cab pickup truck traveling at a high rate of speed. In the third lane, there was an 18-

wheeler. It looked like I was going to collide with that 18-wheeler and that was certainly a very frightening possibility for me, as my car would not stop. However, I prayed to the God of Heaven, and in the name of Jesus, I asked him to spare me, to help me. He did, and he marvelously helped in all kinds of ways. He helped stop the traffic. I know this because after my car eventually came to a stop I looked down the freeway and all across the lanes of the freeway and discovered that multiple lanes of cars had stopped. If they had not, I would have continued to be hit. Angels pushed me out of the way of the 18-wheeler and when other angels simultaneously sent a signal to all of the drivers of all those cars to stop.

Eyewitnesses later told me that when I went across those first two lanes in each lane, I almost got broadsided by a high-speed vehicle, but they slammed on their brakes and they were each able to barely avoid hitting me. I know that I was a benefactor of divine angelic intervention. I sustained massive soft tissue injuries that took years to heal and I had two corrective surgeries, but I didn't lose a limb nor come out paralyzed.

To be honest with you, I was afraid to drive at all for a while.

It took 17 months before I started driving again, and that is because someone gave me a car due to my previous car being a total loss and because I had been hired to substitute teach in a district with schools spread over 46 square miles.

Even so, I was very afraid, very

much afraid of driving on freeways. I remember once that I had to go to a hotel where I had a reservation for the night. And it was conceivably 30 minutes away, but I kept stopping, exiting the freeway, going inside different convenience stores to get snacks, and parking in their parking lots before getting back on the freeway. Since I kept having to rebuild my courage at numerous intervals, it took about 4 hours for me to travel to a place 30 minutes away. I am a living witness that sometimes you have to do things while afraid. When I was driving on the freeway I was praying, I was crying a little bit, I was quoting scriptures, I was talking to God constantly and asking God to help me. And when certain cars came up behind me and they were going faster than I wanted to drive, I sought the Lord to help me by having the high-speed cars move over to the next lane.

Soon, I saw the fruits of my prayers. I know that he helped me through that process and helped me drive in that heavy traffic. At one juncture there was a certain freeway that I wanted to avoid because I knew from driving on it before my accident that people drove very fast. You could even hear the wind sheer that their cars created as they sped through. I had to briefly use that freeway. It was unavoidable. While overcoming my fears mile by mile I had to actually traverse that particular freeway. But I did it while afraid.

What is your thing? Think about it. Then ask yourself, what is the thing in the distant past that you were afraid of but now are no longer afraid of and haven't even thought about in a long time?

Think about your childhood. A lot of children are afraid of things that don't exist; such as something in the closet, something under the bed, monsters, ghosts, or the boogie man. Some are afraid of things that do exist, such as clowns or the dark. If this describes your childhood, chances are you eventually grew out of that fear. What was it that helped you grow out of that? Was it something practical like saying a mantra to yourself as you went forward, or did you grab a bat, did you dash across the floor at lightning speed, and flip the switch to turn on the bathroom light as soon you stepped across the threshold in the bathroom?

Was it something spiritual; such as prayer, or quoting a scripture verse about fear?

Some children and adults are even afraid of getting shots. One of my sisters was that way when we were young. There are plenty of videos of children and adults expressing extreme fear before getting a shot. A lot of people had to get different shots during Covid. If you got the Covid vaccines and boosters, did you have any fear of shots; whether it was fear that they hadn't spent enough time developing those shots before putting them on the market or fear of the temporary pain the needle stick would cause?

Key Verses:

Ezra 3:3a – "Even though they were afraid of what their non-Israelite neighbors might do, they went ahead anyway…"

Ezra 3:10-11 - indicate that the workers laid the Temple's foundation and the people praised God. "All the people boomed out hurrahs, praising God as the foundation of the Temple of God was laid."

Ezra 3:4,11 – "They also celebrated the Festival of Booths as prescribed and the daily Whole-Burnt Offerings set for each day."

What is it in your life that right now you are having trouble doing, and you realize that you ultimately have to do it afraid? The child that is afraid of the dark and has to get up in the middle of the night and go to the restroom is doing it afraid because their bladder is signaling that it's full.

The thing that so easily besets you of which you're afraid - what is it?

What would be your approach for doing it afraid? Take an honest look at the things in your life that hold you back because of fear.

Some people don't know it but if you are dreading something like some dishes in the sink or laundry to do and you want to avoid it, delay it, or you do other things instead. Perhaps you deliberately devote your energy elsewhere or don't even want to look in the direction of that dreaded thing because it will remind you it's yet undone. Even if it's just one or a couple of such things where you are demonstrating dread, you should know that it is a very, very, very close cousin to fear. Is there something that you actually dread and didn't realize was fear operating in your life? What is that one thing that you dread? Is it washing dishes, doing the laundry, or taking out the trash? Is it going to the mailbox, working on a project, doing an assignment, completing something at work, or doing something for your family? Think about that.

I wrote this chapter with two aims – one is to help you to see where your fear or fears might lie. If you take an honest assessment and recognize that possibly there are several things that you fear, or a couple of things that you fear, or even if it's just a single thing that you fear you have to act upon that fear with Holy boldness.

You have the Word of God to help you to overcome your fears. Fears can most definitely be limiting, as you know. I want to stimulate you to look at the scriptural arsenal that we have available to us to help us combat fear.

Your homework assignment before you go to the next chapter, is to identify things that you fear or that you dread. Write those things down and then find scriptures that deal with fear and write those down. After that start meditating daily on those scriptures. Begin to declare and decree them, inserting your name or yourself in those scriptures, like the following example: "God has not given me a spirit of fear…"

I also wrote this chapter with a secondary aim – helping you learn to celebrate integrals of accomplishment.

The second part of your homework is to look at things that you are in the process of accomplishing, but have not finished, sort of like that foundation for the Temple of God in the book of Ezra. Is there a way that you can celebrate the intervals of that instead of waiting until full completion? That would be the next part of your assignment - to answer that question regarding the intervals of completion to celebrate. As you strive to identify intervals that you think are worth celebrating, consider the possibility that they could very well tie into the first part of your homework assignment. It doesn't have to. If you choose to tie in these two parts, then your celebration might be the finishing step of overcoming fear in some areas.

Celebration milestones at certain intervals such as halfway through, or a quarter of the way and onward through might work for this assignment. Next, I want you to plan specifically how you're going to celebrate. Another way of thinking of it is this - How would you reward yourself for getting as far as you have in the project? How would you reward yourself at an even greater level when you finish?

Plan some type of celebration for achieving the milestones, celebrate just as you decided, and then get back to work finishing it with excellence. Stop at each pre-determined interval and then celebrate the completion in some elevated way that exceeds your celebration of the intervals.

Homework
Growth Assignment

Date_____

For whatever was written in earlier times was written for our instruction, so that through endurance and the encouragement of the Scriptures we might have hope and overflow with confidence in His promises.

Romans 15:4 (AMP)

Chapter 7

Revival/Revelations

In this chapter, I want to highlight Ezra and his role in re-establishing worship once again. Even though this is coming out of the book of Nehemiah, his work was tied closely with Ezra as emphasized previously. Let's focus for a minute on Nehemiah 8:1. Here it says, "By the time of the seventh month arrived, the people of Israel were settled in their towns. It goes on to say that all the people gathered as one person in the town square in front of the Water Gate and asked the scholar Ezra to bring the Book of Revelation given by Moses that God had commanded for Israel. Verse 2-3 details how he read to all capable of understanding, from early dawn until noon."

As the people listened, they attended to what he was saying. Verse 3 says they were all ears and verse 5 states that all eyes were on him. It goes on and tells who flanked him on both sides. Verses 5-6 detail how he was standing on an elevated platform, and that as he opened the book everyone stood. You still see this pattern followed in many churches today where, when it's time to read, everyone who is capable is asked to stand.

Then Ezra praised God, the great God, and all the people responded, "Oh, Yes! Yes!", with hands raised high. "And then they fell to their knees in worship of God, their faces to the ground."

My aim in this chapter is to help

you to see the importance of a proper God-honoring approach, protocol, and heart posture to praise and worship and the reading of scripture. Whatever kind of relationship that we have with the Lord, we can probably find ways to improve upon our time of praise and worship, and our time of reading the word of God. I don't mean that as a criticism, but I know that we have busy, demanding lives. Many times, if you're not careful, you'll find that you are short-changing your time of prayer, worship, and Bible reading. I confess that I have been guilty of that myself.

Pearls of Wisdom:

I want to point out another pearl of wisdom. Romans 15:4 says, "For everything that was written in the past was written to teach us, so that through the endurance taught in the Scriptures and the encouragement they provide we might have hope." (NIV) As for the Nehemiah passages that I read, these people started to weep. If you look further into the 8th chapter in verse 9 of the book of Nehemiah it details how Nehemiah, along with Ezra the scholar and the Levites worked in unity. This team of men was teaching the people by reading and then explaining what was read. As for the people, they were listening with respect.

The dynamic trio said to all the people in verses 9-10, "This day is holy to God, your God, don't weep and carry on." They said this because all of the people were weeping as they heard the words of the revelation. He continued in verse 10, "Go home and prepare a feast, holiday food, and drink, and share it with those who don't have anything. This day is holy to God. Don't feel bad. The joy of the Lord is your strength."

A pearl of wisdom here is that we sometimes don't know that something is a blessing when it is. But with help and insight with the desire to be rightly aligned you began to see that it was a blessing like the Israelites did.

One other positive point is that if it doesn't seem like a blessing on the front end, Romans 8:28 tells us that all things work together for the good of them that love the Lord and are called according to His purpose.

How can you raise your attention level on the spiritual things in your life? What do your praise, your worship, and your reading of the word look like right now? What can you do to jump-start a better worship, praise, and Bible reading experience? How can you elevate these things? What new habit or practice can you commit to writing right now and implementing today?

Consider those things where you want to have a better, more optimum time; such as praise and worship. How can you optimize your Bible Reading? This might seem like a repetition from chapter one of this book, but it's not.

The homework that I want you to do before going on to the next chapter is as follows: Examine your praise and worship. Discover where you could improve. In some cases, it's the amount of time you devote to worship or reading the Bible.

I also want you to look again at where distractions need to be eliminated. One specific way that you can improve your time of praise and worship is to make sure that your heart posture is right. Look at whether you need to do any repenting when you pray. Make sure that you are not too critical of yourself or too lenient. By all means, make sure you also listen during prayer. Some say that your prayer time should be about 50% listening, and 50% speaking. Others say that, since you have 1 mouth and 2 ears, you should listen twice as much as you speak. Find what works for you by tuning your spiritual antenna.

Write down your personal spiritual revival plan and then implement it.

Homework
Growth Assignment

Date_____

For whatever was written in earlier times was written for our instruction, so that through endurance and the encouragement of the Scriptures we might have hope and overflow with confidence in His promises.

Romans 15:4 (AMP)

Chapter 8

History

In this chapter, I want to talk about history; more specifically when it's relevant to look back at your own acts. In Chapter 1 of this book, I mentioned that Ezra had received permission, resources, and everything that he needed to go and rebuild the Temple of God as well as to re-institute worship by the people of Israel. However, if we look at Ezra chapter 5 verses 11-13, we will find that them having to explain to some of the leaders why they are rebuilding the temple and they tell them, "We are servants of the God of the Heavens and the Earth. We are rebuilding the temple that was built a long time ago. A great king of Israel built it, the entire structure, but our ancestors made the God of the heavens really angry. And he turned them over to Nebuchadnezzar, king of Babylon, the Chaldean, who knocked this temple down. And took the people to Babylon in exile."

The proceeding verses explain that King Cyrus had issued a building permit and had given everything that Ezra needed to rebuild and to re-institute worship.

Let's take a look at our own lives. When you meditate on your history with God try searching for things that God has allowed you to go through such as troubles, tribulations, and even the chastening of the Lord. Be honest about whether at the time and afterward whether you found yourself not experiencing the full favor of God because of your choices.

What I mean is a full close relationship with God. It's not that he has moved away, but that he may be allowing you to experience some consequences for wrong decisions and actions - just as he did with the Israelites. They were the apple of his eye, but they continued to rebel and disobey. They continued to go their own way and forgot about his faithfulness numerous times, and eventually, he did give them over to King Nebuchadnezzar, the King of Babylon.

Have you ever taken God's goodness and grace for granted in a similar way?

Ask yourself where you might have experienced something like this. Try to pinpoint what the process of being restored was like. What does/did that look like for you? Next, I want you to ask yourself when God chastened you, or when you went through the trials and tribulations and then came out of them were you still tempted to go right back to your own vomit? Were you still tempted to rebel, to be disobedient? Or were you committed to the right pathway going forward? Be honest.

A positive point if you've strayed: God has promised that we can be restored to him. He will cast our sins behind his back (Isaiah 39:17), but we have to really be sincere and turn away from sin. Repentance as it is described and defined by the Oxford Online Dictionary is an action that involves deep regret, and sincere remorse for something one has done. It also involves turning away from that sin. Is not just asking for forgiveness for something, but turning away from it and going in a different direction.

Try to recall what you did after God stopped the chastening, or put an end to the trials and tribulations. For that season after your chastening, or whatever, how did you live going forward from that experience? He tells us that we can always be restored, and he will always forgive. So, if you were one of those people that chose to get back on the wrong pathway after God began to restore you there is a solution. Some action steps to return to the joy of the Lord.

Key Verses:

Nehemiah 10:29b – "...everyone old enough to understand – all joined their noble kinsmen in a binding oath to follow the Revelation of God given through Moses the servant of God, to keep and carry out all the commandments of God our Master, all his decisions and standards."

Nehemiah 8:10b – "The joy of the Lord is your strength."

Number 1. You can always change your mind and change your actions and go back the right way.

Number 2. You're in good company because, unfortunately, as you continue looking in the book of Ezra there were other times that they rebelled again while fresh out of exile. This included marrying women that were not of their faith.

You will see that in Ezra chapter 9, verses 1-2. Then if you look at the verses after, you will see how Ezra prayed intercessory prayers and even ripped his clothes and his cape and pulled his hair out of his head and from his beard. It really broke his heart to see that they were just acting just like they had before God allowed them to experience Babylonian captivity and then took them out of that captivity. In Nehemiah, chapter 9: 20b; 27, Nehemiah described God by saying, "You were never miserly with your manna," and, "And in keeping with your bottomless compassion." In verse 28 he said, "But as soon as they had it easy again they were right back at it - more evil."

Since you are in good company if you've fallen short and lived as if the lesson didn't "take," don't feel condemned, because God does not condemn you. Look at how he showed mercy to the Israelites over and over again. Look at what he said to the woman at the well, as recounted in John 8:11. "Neither do I condemn you, go and sin no more." This lets us know that we can stop, and we can go another direction, and we can be restored.

The next thing that I want you to take a look at is what are your proper action steps for being restored. I can give you an example from my own life.

I recall how, in my early adulthood, when I was in a very abusive marriage and was still in that marriage, I found that it wasn't getting any better. It finally escalated to the point where I thought that I could be killed in the presence of my tween son. I remember when, in one of my darkest moments, a friend called me. I answered the phone and she gave me a scripture. I hung on to that scripture like it was a lifeline, and indeed it was.

I came to realize something after I was divorced; God brought me out of that marriage. I realized that I played a key part in getting into that fix. I saw that marrying a non-believer was my first act of disobedience. I owned the fact that the things I experienced in that marriage were part and parcel consequences of my disobedience for marrying a non-believer. He apparently did not love himself so he could not love me. People can only give you what they have.

Going from there, I had to be restored to fellowship with the Lord, then to the church. I re-dedicated my life to God. The reason I took those steps is because at some point in my marriage, I blamed God for what I was going through and I stopped going to church, and I spent my Sundays like the heathens do. I stayed at home, watched TV, went shopping, I had my hair done or my nails or whatever I would do on any other day. I was not honoring the Sabbath as holy and consecrated because I felt forsaken by God. In terms of my lifestyle, I didn't go into full rebellion - I wasn't out there drinking and smoking or doing drugs.

It wasn't anything like that, I just simply ceased pursuing an active relationship with the Lord and attending church. When I started attending church again and rededicated my life to Christ, I went all in. I chose not to look back, because the abundant life that I was experiencing was still not perfect, but it was significantly better. I was excited about all of the things of God. I was excited about everything; from knowing him personally, to having a prayer life again, to finding so much light and direction from his word. I was even going out and witnessing to others, trying to bring others into the kingdom, which is The Great Commission for all Christians.

I made sure that my son was attending church and Sunday School regularly. My son was also involved in the church youth group and even the youth choir. I attended really awesome Bible studies both at my church and one outside of my church, which was Bible Study Fellowship (BSF). Bible Study Fellowship uses a 4-fold approach to systematic Bible studies in various group formations.

Enough about me. What kind of intentionality are you showing toward being restored after whatever it was that required restoration? What are your plans and action steps?

Your homework before going to the next chapter is to write down your steps for restoration. At the bottom, write and then sign an oath to commit to going forward with an appreciation for God's history of faithfulness to you. Make sure the steps are in writing, by sequence. Your next step is to do them. For most people, repentance should be the first step.

Refer back to my example:

- Joining a Bible-believing, Jesus-exalting church

- Faithfully planting myself in that church

- Joining the choir and attending rehearsals and services

- Rededication of my life to God

- Getting into a corporate Bible study

- Studying the Word at home.

You are welcome to copy my pattern and rearrange/edit/cater it specifically to your life (for instance, maybe you are not a singer, but an usher, teacher, etc.). I didn't get baptized again, but that could be something you'd like to add.

Whatever your steps and sequence look like, be sure to follow them faithfully unless you are led by God to make modifications.

Homework
Growth Assignment

Date_____

For whatever was written in earlier times was written for our instruction, so that through endurance and the encouragement of the Scriptures we might have hope and overflow with confidence in His promises.

Romans 15:4 (AMP)

Chapter 9

Diligence/Due Diligence

In this chapter I want to highlight the steadfast work demonstrated throughout the chapter duo. In Nehemiah 4:6, after Nehemiah prayed to God upon discovering that their enemies were insulting the builders, it is recorded that they pressed on. "We kept at it, repairing and rebuilding the wall. The whole wall was soon joined together and halfway to its intended height, because the people had a heart for the work." Another way of saying that people had a heart for the work is to say that people were diligent. If you were to look up the definition of diligent you would find words that indicate being steadfast and unmovable and devoted to doing quality work and not being idle. Today, we refer to it as having a "strong work ethic." The Cambridge Dictionary Online defines work ethic as, "The belief that work is valuable as an activity and is morally good."

Today we sometimes hear people talk about taking mental health days off from work. This is where they take off work for reasons other than being sick or needing to keep an appointment. It could involve a day of just chilling at home watching movies or doing other non-essential things. I have to admit that I've taken such days myself. That practice certainly didn't come from the books of Ezra and Nehemiah.

Take a moment to ask yourself whether you are diligent at your tasks - be it on a job, at home, in your own business, etc. Where are you showing diligence?

I would like you to think either about your job or your business or your ministry as relates to diligence. If you're a Sunday school teacher, describe yourself and how you're diligent in that role. Do you study the intended scripture verses before you get to church? Do you pre-plan a lesson or some activities that help support the lesson? If this is where most of your diligence can be shown, what capacities are assigned to you if you're a housewife? How do you approach this? I believe being a housewife is both wonderful and honorable. How are you diligent at that role? If you are a caregiver, how are you diligent at that role? There's been many news reports of caregivers leaving babies and children unattended while they go to a shopping center. In one instance the children perished in a fire. I've heard of the elderly in extended care facilities being neglected, abused and ill-treated.

Think about this while bearing in mind that God sees everything we do, or fail to do. Do you work as though He is looking over your shoulder? Do you do your work with diligence and excellence?

Key Verse:

Neh. 4:6 (emphasis mine) "We kept at it repairing and building the wall. The whole wall was soon joined together and halfway to its intended height **because the people had a heart for the work.**"

Where are you giving due diligence? This term is defined by Cambridge as, "Action that is considered reasonable for people to be expected to take in order to keep themselves or others and their property safe." In the construction industry, where my son is employed, people wear hard hats, steel-toed boots and other safety equipment.

If there's something that you need to do; such as form an LLC for your business, due diligence would look like this: You research with the Secretary of State most likely in the state where the business is operated. You would call or go to the state website to find out whether the name that you want to use for your business is available. You don't want to take the name of another entity, especially one in the same industry.

Due diligence would be finding out where and how to file for your LLC versus casually clicking on an LLC formation website and beginning their filing process. You'd want to find out the benefits/protections or the pros and cons of filing an LLC, and how much it would cost, what add-ons your state requires, etc. In some states, other people need to be involved in that process for you to form that LLC. You will do due diligence and find out which specialist(s) is/are needed and then vet the candidates by checking reviews and testimonials of their former clients, verifying their credentials and possibly doing a background check. As I am not an attorney, I can't dispense legal advice. I just want to use this example to show what due diligence should look like.

Another example of due diligence might occur if you were seeking to know about school your children will attend when you move to another location, city, state or country. You can go online to Great Schools and research some of the specifics of each school, by name. You can ask for a tour of a potential school, particularly during a school day if feasible.

You might talk to other parents that send their child to that school and discover what they think, or what their experiences have been like, or whether they would recommend it.

Likewise, before you move to a new location you might want to go on Crime Databases in the intended area to see the latest crime statistics by type.

Due diligence could include looking into references or checking reviews, or checking testimonials from the others who have visited or supported a business, or signed up for something, like a certain bank; or it could be programs like recreational programs that you're considering; or something else in which you want to invest energy, time or money.

I remember once before I moved into a neighborhood that I wasn't familiar with, there was an apartment complex I considered moving into. I visited during different times of the day and I drove by to see whether they had the police there all the time, whether it was noisy, whether the dumpsters were overflowing with trash and debris. Those are red flags that I would look for. I didn't see any red flags and there seemed to be good energy around that place, so I signed the lease and moved in.

Key Verses:

<u>Neh. 2:13,15</u> "Under cover of night I went past the Valley Gate towards the Dragon's Fountain to the Dung Gate looking over the walls of Jerusalem, which had been broken through and whose gate had been burned up." "So I went up the valley in the dark continuing my inspection of the wall."

Pearl of Wisdom:

Sometimes our due diligence should be done in the dark and/or in secret. In Nehemiah 2:16 the cupbearer recounts, "I hadn't breathed a word to the Jews, priests, nobles, local officials, or anyone else who would be working on the job."

Think about due diligence. Where do you need to do due diligence, do some digging, conduct some research? A positive point that I want to share is that diligence and due diligence should be your portion. Those are areas where you can grow and increase as you practice them over time. If you realize you're not as diligent as you should be at something, you can always figure out how you can become more diligent.

I want you to now face your attention on these things: What would someone else say about how diligent you are? I'm talking someone like a supervisor a business partner. I'm not talking about somebody just random, but the people that matter - whether it's the owner of the company where you work, or your manager, or your principal, your supervisor, or someone that you report to who also is the one that can recommend you for raises and appraises/

observes/evaluates your work, or could serve as a future reference. What would they have to say about your diligence on the job?

Due diligence would dictate that you find out in advance what criterion they would use to measure your job performance? You need to know this ahead of time so you can address those areas through implementation, taking a training course or practicing.

I want to provoke you toward continuous improvement in the things assigned to your hands. My prayer is that you don't fall into a state of laxity. I'm not saying that things should be done perfectly or look perfect. I'm saying, are you doing things with the spirit of excellence? Is there a high standard that you aim for in areas of your life?

Your homework before going to the next chapter is to think about, through prayer and seeking God, what is a strategy that you can use for victory born of diligence in a particular area - such as on your job, in your business, in your home, in your relationships? Write down actions that will make you more diligent. It could even be strategies of diligence that will make you better, or that will help you to overcome enemies, or that will help you to show more fidelity to duty.

Next, I want you to write down anything on your schedule for the next six months that will require due diligence. Ask God for specific due diligence strategies to address the anticipated activities. Be sure to write down the date you asked.

I am assigning one specific due diligence finance-related task, but you can choose the others on your own. There is an increasing high number of people stealing money by inserting fake card readers and keypads on top of the one the bank or store provides. I want you to perform due diligence and find out ways that you can avoid having your money taken digitally or otherwise through fake credit card skimmers when you're at an ATM, store or gas pump. Write down the recommended practices (usually found on legitimate news sites and at banks or bank websites). Be sure to implement those cautionary practices on a faithful basis. Next, I would love for you to share the results of your research with a family member, friend or loved one. As mentioned before, the other areas for this assignment are at your discretion.

Regarding the other areas of your choosing, when you receive what you asked for, write down the date that it manifests and how it manifests. I believe God is faithful and will give you glorious victories. I pray that you won't jump into something without doing due diligence so you won't have to invest a massive amount of time/effort/money to repair the damage.

Homework
Growth Assignment

Date_____

For whatever was written in earlier times was written for our instruction, so that through endurance and the encouragement of the Scriptures we might have hope and overflow with confidence in His promises.

Romans 15:4 (AMP)

Chapter 10

My Worship is the Real Deal

The main things I want to talk about in this chapter are how to engage in true worship based on your personal history with God, dedication to His way of worship, and strategy. As mentioned in an earlier chapter, strategy can be defined as a method or system for doing something or accomplishing something. From the book of Nehemiah we can see that with prayer, Nehemiah was able to receive ideas and strategies to help with the rebuilding project. He executed them with excellence.

The 4th chapter of Nehemiah, verses 13 and 14 recount after they had experienced some reports that their dedicated enemies were saying certain things and even gathering around them; some trying to surround them to attack. He reports, "It is so I stationed armed guards at the most vulnerable places of the wall. And assigned people by families with their swords, lances and bows, after looking over things I stood up and spoke to the nobles, officials, and everyone, don't be afraid of them. Put your mind on the master Great and awesome, and then fight for your brothers, your sons, your daughters, your wives and your homes.

Let's focus for a minute on Nehemiah 8 verse 1. Here it says that by the time the seventh month arrived, the people of Israel were settled in their towns. It goes on to say that all the people gathered as one person in the town square in front of the Water Gate and asked the scholar Ezra to bring the Book of Revelation given by Moses that God had commanded for Israel. Verse 2-3 details how he read to all capable of understanding, from early dawn until noon.

As the people listened, they attended to what he was saying. Verse 3 says they were all ears and verse 5 states that all eyes were on him. Verses 5-6 detail how he was standing on an elevated platform, and that as he opened the book everyone stood. Then Ezra praised God, the great God, and all the people responded, "Oh, Yes! Yes!", with hands raised high. And then they fell to their knees in worship of God, their faces to the ground."

I know I am repeating some scripture and details from a previous chapter, but I am leading you to a different area of focus. This chapter somewhat piggybacks off of the one right before it (Chapter 7: History).

My aim in this chapter is to help you to see the importance of taking your oaths and commitments to God seriously. If we take them seriously, we will have more fruitful times with the Lord, and you will see that it is not burdensome.

Pearls of Wisdom:

I want to point out another pearl of wisdom. Romans 15:4 says, "For everything that was written in the past was written to teach us, so that through the endurance taught in the Scriptures and the encouragement they provide we might have hope." (NIV)

Key Verses:

Nehemiah 10:29: "Everyone made an oath to follow God."

John 4: 23-24: "It's who you are and the way you live that count before God. Your worship must engage your spirit in the pursuit of truth. That's the kind of people the Father is out looking for: those who are simply and honestly themselves before him in their worship. God is sheer being itself—Spirit. Those who worship him must do it out of their very being, their spirits, their true selves, in adoration." (ESV)

You should look at how well you follow the oaths you've made to God. Have you made a commitment to worship Him the way he deserves to be worshiped? Are your eyes and ears attentive to sermons, messages, prayers, worship, and praise?

The homework that I want you to do as you close out this book is to listen to any version of the song, "My Worship is for Real," by Bishop Larry Trotter. Next, I want you to listen a second time to a version that includes the lyrics and write them down on your Homework Growth Assignment page. As long as you use the song lyrics for your personal use in your private time alone, you are not violating copyright laws.

Read the lyrics out loud daily and consider whether your own worship is the real deal. If you find that it's not, write down 2 things that you can do going forward to be a more genuine worshiper using the key verses mentioned earlier in this chapter and the lyrics of the song.

The next step is to bind yourself by writing down your own personal oath to follow God in some specific way. Be certain to promise something you can fulfill such as praying as soon as you awake each day, getting up early to pray, having private times of worship with God, or reading your Bible for a certain number of minutes per day (with a study plan). If you make an oath within your capabilities and commit to it, you are not swearing deceitfully. Next, read that oath out loud on a daily basis and assess for yourself how you are doing at keeping that oath.

Homework
Growth Assignment

Date_____

 Writezous Publishing

Shirley A. Franklin
Editor-in-Chief

To see other teaching materials developed by this author visit the following websites:

Teachers Pay Teachers:

https://www.teacherspayteachers.com/Store/Shirley-Franklin

Etsy (Teacher Treasures):

https://teactreasures.etsy.com/

Author Contact and Booking Information:
Email: educatorinstructorteacher@gmail.com
Local #: 512-337-8332
Toll-free #: 1-888-850-7479
Instagram: @shirleya.franklin

Other Books:

"Aunt Juicy's Wayward Family" is available on Thrift Books by following the QR code below:

Review for "Aunt Juicy's Wayward Family": https://www.instagram.com/p/CtS17GQSotW/?igshid=MzRlODBiNWFlZA==

If you enjoyed using this book, please provide a review on Amazon.com, Goodreads, and Library Thing!

The companion to this book - "One Hand to Build, One Hand to Fight: Being a Christian Teacher of Love, Light and Spiritual Might" is also available wherever books are sold.

www.ingramcontent.com/pod-product-compliance
Lightning Source LLC
Chambersburg PA
CBHW071929290426
44110CB00013B/1531